THE LI

TO

TIPS

ANDREW LANGLEY

THE LITTLE BOOK OF TOAST TIPS

ANDREW LANGLEY

A.
Absolute Press

First published in Great Britain in 2013 by
Absolute Press, an imprint of Bloomsbury Publishing Plc
Scarborough House, 29 James Street West
Bath BA1 2BT, England
Phone +44 (0)1225 316013 **Fax** +44 (0)1225 445836
E-mail info@absolutepress.co.uk
Web www.absolutepress.co.uk

A catalogue record of this book is available from the British Library
ISBN 13: 9781906650926
Printed and bound by Hung Hing, China.

Bloomsbury Publishing Plc
50 Bedford Square, London WC1B 3DP | www.bloomsbury.com

'The smell of that buttered toast simply talked to Toad, and with no uncertain voice; talked of warm kitchens, of breakfasts on bright frosty mornings, of cosy parlour firesides on winter evenings, of the purring of contented cats.'

Kenneth Grahame (1859–1932),
Scottish writer,
from *The Wind in the Willows*

1

Fresh bread makes the best toast. Traditionally, toasting was a handy way of making stale bread tastier. But a slice of fresh has more moisture and elasticity – not to mention flavour.. When toasted, it has that seductive combination of crisp outside and soft inside which is irresistible.

2

The better the bread, the better the toast.

Wholemeal, white, sourdough, three seed, malted, baguette – anything will produce splendid toast as long as it's well made with good quality ingredients and as few additives as possible. If it's home-made, even better. Spurn all mass-produced sliced stuff with global brand names.

3

How thick should a slice of toast be?

Too thin (like most ready-sliced), and there won't be enough doughy elastic inside to contrast with the crunchy toasted outside. Too thick, and the soft:hard ratio is reversed. Between half and three-quarters of an inch (1½–2cm) should give the ideal balance.

4

A scientist has calculated that

216 seconds is the optimum toasting period

for your average slice. That's about 3½ minutes – which gives a fifteen second overlap at each end for you to start and finish boiling an egg to perfection. (Stop watch optional.)

5

Be choosy when you buy a toaster.

So what are you looking for? It should brown the bread evenly on both sides (hard to predict, admittedly). It should be simple to operate (you're mostly using it first thing in the morning). And it should have nice wide slots (so thicker slabs of toast don't get stuck).

6

No toaster? That's no problem.

Just heat olive oil to a medium heat in a skillet or frying pan. Rub one side of a slice of bread in the pan to soak up some of the oil, then turn over and cook the other side till golden. Flip over and fry the first side ditto. Watch carefully to be sure it doesn't scorch.

7

Remember to **clean out your toaster regularly.** Piles of old breadcrumbs soon clog up the bottom of it, getting staler and blacker, and tending to shed themselves all over the worktop. A good toaster should have a drawer or similar which can be easily extracted and emptied. A brush will drag out the clingier particles.

8

Bread toasted on a real wood fire may get a little burned sometimes, but it's **worth it for the smoky tang.** Make sure the fire is well established, with good solid hardwood embers which you can rake together. Avoid toasting over smoke (which will ruin the taste) or flames (which will just burn the bread).

9

Use a proper toasting fork before a live fire rather than improvising with kitchen forks or worse. The fork should have tines which are slightly curved at the ends. Insert these firmly into the bread at an upward angle, otherwise the slice may slip off into the fire.

10

Butter fresh toast immediately once it is ready. Sounds obvious, but the hotter the toast the quicker the butter will melt. Toast left to stand about will soon go leathery and lose its heat, so the butter may not melt at all, but just get smeared about.

11

Serve toast on a plate which is ready-warmed.

A cold plate will cause the escaping moisture to condense, making the bottom of the toast soggy. A warm one will avoid this disaster (although if it's too hot the toast will overcook).

12

Croutons, made with care, **brighten up any soup or salad.**

Peel garlic cloves and rub them into slices of day-old baguette (which should be hard enough to act like graters). Cut the slices into cubes and toast them in hot olive oil until they are golden. Sprinkle on the salad or soup just before serving.

13

Great garlic bread

needs just three ingredients. A slice of bread, a layer of olive oil (butter if you must) and a sprinkling of crushed garlic. Lay on an oiled baking sheet and bake in a hot oven (220°C) for a maximum of ten minutes – until it's golden brown.

14

There's **an even more heavenly garlic bread experience.**

Simmer 10 peeled garlic cloves for 5 minutes in water, then drain and fry gently in butter. Mash the result and mix into $1/4$ pint (150ml) of prepared and warmed bechamel sauce. Spread on toast, sprinkle with breadcrumbs and crisp up under the grill.

15

The Italian word *bruscare* means 'to toast'.

Hence **bruscheta,**

which is just toasted bread. Its

most basic and magical form

requires slices of good country Italian bread with a thick crust, toasted golden on a grill. Rub one side with a peeled garlic clove (or mashed garlic), drizzle on good olive oil and season with pepper and salt.

16

Bruschetta demands one other ingredient: tomato. The Italians de-seed and finely chop them, and flavour with torn basil leaves before heaping the mixture on top. The Catalans, in their more earthy way, simply cut the tomatoes in half and rub the cut sides on the toast. They call this *pan amb tomat* (bread and tomato).

17

Pâté is **another authentically traditional topping for bruschetta.**

Buy a high-quality chicken liver pâté or, better still, make your own. Sauté the washed and chopped livers with shallots in oil, deglaze with *vin santo* and thyme, then purée. Spread generously on the toasted bread.

18

Another classic way with bruschetta.

Strictly speaking, this is a recipe for *crostini neri* (black crostini), but who's arguing? Chop 220g of stoned black olives and 4 anchovy fillets, then whizz into a paste with olive oil and a handful of capers. Season to taste and spread on the freshly toasted bread.

19

The ultimate bruschetta is actually Mallorcan. Modestly called *pa amb oli* (bread and oil) it is without doubt a meal in itself. On a base of *pan amb tomat* (see Tip #16), pile olives, capers and pickled peppers, plus slices of local cheese, Serrano ham and Mallorcan sausage such as *sobrasada*. Serve with a green salad.

20

Melba toast is the perfect vehicle for pâté. Slice white bread thinly – about 7mm. Toast on both sides by placing as close to the grill as you can (avoid burning it). Immediately cut off the crusts and split each piece in half horizontally. Cut into triangles and toast further away from the grill for 30 seconds or less.

21

How do you make **perfect fried bread?** Olive oil, butter or bacon fat are fine for the frying medium, but best of all is goose fat. Be sparing – a teaspoon is plenty for one slice. Melt in a frying pan at high heat, coat one side and turn over. After a minute, turn again and leave another minute. Dab with kitchen paper to remove excess oil.

22

There's a fine art to cutting

toast soldiers for dipping into your boiled egg.

Too thick, and they won't fit into the egg. Too thin, and you risk the laden end falling back into the yolk. So make them at least half an inch (12mm) square, and use a good solid bread like sourdough which won't disintegrate under pressure.

23

These **cheesy toasts** are not just soldiers – they're special forces. Place bread fingers (cut as in preceding tip) in a bowl. Pour on a mixture of melted **butter and Dijon mustard,** season, **and** sprinkle with grated **cheese** (gruyere or pecorino), plus a little thyme. Spread the fingers on a tray and bake in a hot oven for about 15 minutes.

24

Feeling weedy and unloved? A bowl of

milk toast is the ultimate comfort food.

Tear up a slice of buttered toast and put in the bowl. Heat up about ¼ pint (140ml) of whole milk till near boiling. Pour it over the toast (the milk can be flavoured with raisins and salt, cinnamon and sugar, or a little nutmeg).

25

If, on the other hand, you're feeling sinful and bold, **treat yourself to condensed milk toast.** Take a good thick slice of a sweetish bread such as chollah or brioche and butter it. Spread on top a generous layer of condensed milk, and pop under the grill for two minutes or a little more.

26

The idea of a **toasted cheese sandwich** seems pretty simple. Here's **a jazzier version.** Assemble the sandwich, with two slices of country bread, slices of cheddar and pear, and some cooked bacon. Butter the top of the sandwich and fry in a pan till golden. Turn over, butter the other side and fry that, pressing down with a spatula.

27

Anyone can make

cheese on toast

– it's exactly what it says. Here's

a slightly more sophisticated take on it. Butter or oil a slice of bread and warm in a hot oven for 3 minutes. Mix together a handful of grated Cheddar cheese and dessert spoons of mayonnaise and French mustard. Spread on the bread and toast in the oven for 5 minutes.

28

The most famous cheese on toast is Welsh rarebit

(or rabbit). Heat 3 tablespoons of Welsh stout with a blob of English mustard and a knob of butter. Then stir in 175g of grated Lancashire cheese and melt together gently. Beat in 2 egg yolks. Spread the result on 2 lightly toasted slices of good solid bread and toast in the oven or under a grill.

29

Croque-monsieur is the king of toasted sandwiches.

Being French, it demands a bechamel sauce, flavoured with melted gruyere. Grill two slices of buttered bread on the buttered side.

Put mustard, ham and more gruyere on one slice and heat to melt the cheese. Press the second slice on top, pour over the sauce and grill for another 5 minutes.

30

Avocado toast is another simple-sounding dish. Just toast some pungent country bread, **drizzle on olive oil, and mash avocado on top,** before grilling the top. Yet even this can be refined. Try adding grated parmesan, or chilli flakes, or cherry tomatoes (quickly sautéed), or a squeeze of lime or lemon, plus lots of black pepper.

31

Here's **the quickest dessert in the world.** Grill slices of crusty white bread, and top immediately with ricotta (fresh, if you can get it) and a spoonful of clear honey (preferably Greek).

32

What's the point of

a toast rack?

Fresh toast gives off steam and, heaped flat, soon goes soggy. A well-designed rack separates the slices and **allows air to circulate** between them, thus avoiding sogginess. However, this quickly cools the toast – so place the rack somewhere warm, like a radiator.

33

Beans on toast we all know, but

how about broad beans on toast?

Parboil the beans for 5 minutes, then stew slowly in olive oil with chopped garlic and either chopped Serrano ham or good quality black pudding for another 30 minutes. Serve on toast with more oil and a scattering of chopped mint or fennel.

34

French toast comes in many guises. In France itself it is known as *pain perdu*, or ‘lost bread’, meaning stale bread which might otherwise be chucked to the hens. Traditionally, the slices are soaked in a mixture of milk and brandy. These are then coated in a floury, milky batter and fried.

35

Eggy bread is the **simple,** English, foolproof, **child-friendly** relative of *pain perdu*. Just beat up 2 or 3 fresh eggs, and dip slices of bread in the mixture until they are well coated. Instantly fry the slices in oil or butter. Tomato ketchup is the mandatory accompaniment.

36

Here's **a de-luxe version of French toast.**

Whisk together 6 eggs, the juice of 2 oranges, 250ml of milk, a drop of vanilla essence and a pinch of salt. Add a teaspoon of orange zest. Coat bread slices in this gunge, then fry in butter (about 2 minutes a side). Serve hot with honey or maple syrup, and maybe some sliced banana.

37

Even more exotic is kaya toast, a favourite from Southeast Asia. Heat 250ml of fresh coconut milk with 8 pandan leaves. Beat together 6 eggs, 250g of sugar and a pinch of salt, and then stir in the coconut milk. When smooth, put through a sieve, then heat gently for 30 minutes, stirring a lot. Allow to cool and spread on buttered toast.

38

Pizza on toast is a worthy shortcut to the real thing – made right.

Grate 6 ripe tomatoes into a pan with oregano and simmer for 20 minutes. Spread over thin slices of a firm, close-crumbed white bread. Grate mozzarella cheese on top, and finish with pepperoni, capers and pitted black olives. Toast in a hot oven for 15 minutes.

39

Egg-in-the-hole

gives you **toast and fried egg** at the same time.

With a scone cutter, cut a hole in the middle of a big slice of wholemeal bread. Toast one side in a little olive oil until golden, then flip over. Break a fresh egg in the hole – it will take as long to cook as the other side of the toast.

40

Cinnamon toast is an old nursery favourite.

The traditional method is laughably simple: butter your toast thickly, then sprinkle on a mixture of sugar and ground cinnamon. For a superior version, turn the sugar/cinnamon mix into a paste by stirring it up with water, milk or – even better – a little red wine. Not for the nursery, this.

41

We toast bread.

The French roast it too – with herbs.

Brush thick slices of stale country bread with olive oil. Sprinkle with the following *herbes de la garrigue*, crushed or milled together: bay leaf, summer savory, basil, sage, rosemary, thyme, marjoram and fennel seed. Roast in a hot oven for just under 10 minutes, till golden.

42

Toasted pitta bread is the base for

a wonderful Lebanese dish called *fattee*.

Cover the bottom of a serving dish with triangles of buttery toasted pitta. On top of this go layers of cooked rice, roast chicken (and its juices), fried aubergine, tomato sauce, yogurt, parsley and toasted pine nuts.

43

The foregoing is easily confused with

another bready delight from the Med – *fattoush*. This is a salad made from sliced red pepper, rocket, tomato, coriander, mint and sumac, mixed with chunks of toasted pitta bread. Toss in a dressing of olive oil, lemon and crushed garlic.

44

How To Make Crumpets 1 of 2: The Batter.

Sift together 225g of each of white bread flour and plain flour, plus a teaspoon of cream of tartar. Froth up some dried yeast in half a litre of bloodwarm water and a dash of sugar. Mix with the flour into a smooth batter, cover and put in a warm place to prove for 1 hour. Then beat in 1 tablespoon of salt.

45

How To Make Crumpets 2 of 2: The Toasting.

Stir in 140ml of lukewarm water mixed with ½ teaspoon of baking soda. Heat and grease a frying pan with a crumpet ring. Spoon in batter to about 1cm thick. Holes should form (if not, adjust the consistency with water or flour). After 7 minutes, flip over and toast for 3 more minutes.

46

Turn that dull breakfast toast into a face – for kids of all ages.

Trim the slice into a circle, then add a sausage for a mouth, tomato halves for ears, mushrooms for eyes, bacon for a fringe, and so on. A dab of ketchup here, a sprig of parsley there, the odd strategically placed baked bean, and you have

a work of art.

47

Here's a candidate for

most sinful toast recipe.

Cut a ciabatta into triangles and split them in half. Spread one lot of halves with a mixture of honey and almond butter, plus pinches of salt and ground cloves. Top with squares of classy dark bitter chocolate, place the other halves on top and bake in a hot oven for 7–10 minutes.

48

Chinese shrimp toasts, or *hatosi*, make brilliant appetisers.

In a processor, whizz up 450g of peeled shrimps with 30g of cornflour, a chopped spring onion, 1 egg, 2 teaspoons of grated ginger, a little chopped ham and seasoning. Spread on fingers of crustless white bread and fry in hot groundnut oil, shrimp side first.

49

Everyone burns the toast sometimes. What to do?

The frugal solution is to scrape off the black layer with the edge of a knife, and carry on as normal. If the toast is beyond redemption, whizz it up as breadcrumbs, mix with some fat or oil and put out for the birds.

50

The charred smell of burnt toast can hang around for days. **Get rid of it** by opening windows or burning candles (yes, they neutralise smells). Put out bowls of vinegar. Sprinkle affected cushions and furnishings with baking soda, leave overnight and vacuum up the next day. Buy some lillies.

Andrew Langley

Andrew Langley is a knowledgeable food and drink writer. Among his formative influences he lists a season picking grapes in Bordeaux, several years of raising sheep and chickens in Wiltshire and two decades drinking his grandmother's tea. He has been an author for over 30 years and was the editor of the highly regarded anthology of the writings of the legendary Victorian chef Alexis Soyer.

THE LITTLE BOOK OF
BARBECUE
TIPS
ANDREW LANGLEY

THE LITTLE BOOK OF
BEER
TIPS
ANDREW LANGLEY

THE LITTLE BOOK OF
HERB
TIPS
WILLIAM FORTT

THE LITTLE BOOK OF
POKER
TIPS

THE LITTLE BOOK OF
GARDENING
TIPS
WILLIAM FORTT

THE LITTLE BOOK OF
CHEFS'
TIPS
RICHARD

THE LITTLE BOOK OF
SPICE
TIPS
ANDREW LANGLEY

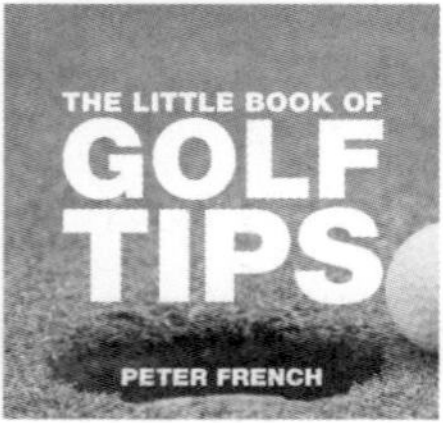
THE LITTLE BOOK OF
GOLF
TIPS
PETER FRENCH

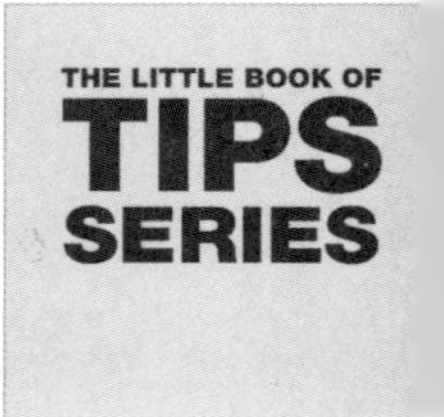
THE LITTLE BOOK OF
TIPS
SERIES

THE LITTLE BOOK OF
CHEESE
TIPS
ANDREW LANGLEY

THE LITTLE BOOK OF
WINE
TIPS
ANDREW LANGLEY

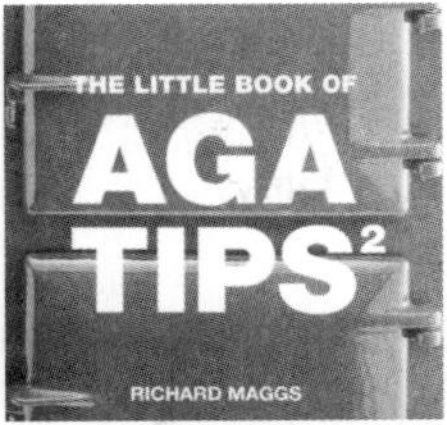
THE LITTLE BOOK OF
AGA
TIPS 2
RICHARD MAGGS

THE LITTLE BOOK OF
COFFEE
TIPS
ANDREW LANGLEY

THE LITTLE BOOK OF
TEA
TIPS
ANDREW LANGLEY

THE LITTLE BOOK OF
AGA
TIPS 3
RICHARD MAGGS

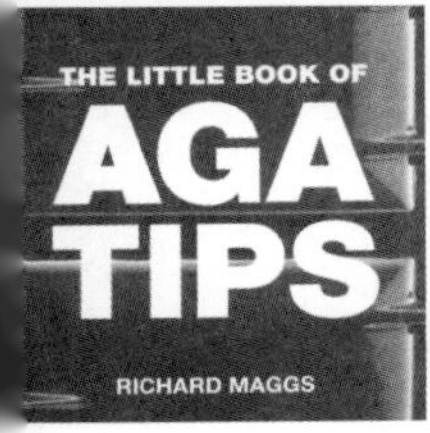
THE LITTLE BOOK OF
AGA
TIPS
RICHARD MAGGS

THE LITTLE BOOK OF
CHRISTMAS
AGA
TIPS
RICHARD MAGGS

THE LITTLE BOOK OF
RAYBURN
TIPS
RICHARD MAGGS

THE LITTLE BOOK OF
BRIDGE
TIPS
PETER FRENCH

THE LITTLE BOOK OF
CHESS
TIPS
PETER FRENCH

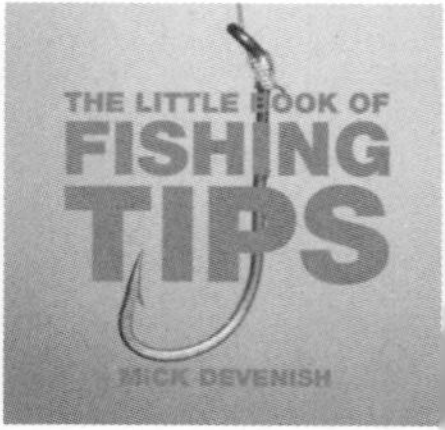
THE LITTLE BOOK OF
FISHING
TIPS
MICK DEVENISH

THE LITTLE BOOK OF
GREEN
TIPS
WILLIAM FORTT

THE LITTLE BOOK OF
KITTEN
TIPS
ANDREW LANGLEY

MARMITE
PAUL HARTLEY
THE LITTLE BOOK OF
MARMITE
TIPS

THE LITTLE BOOK OF
PUPPY
TIPS
ANDREW LANGLEY

THE LITTLE BOOK OF
WHISKY
TIPS
ANDREW LANGLEY

THE LITTLE BOOK OF
TRAVEL
TIPS
MEGAN DEVENISH

Little Books of Tips from Absolute Press

Aga Tips
Aga Tips 2
Aga Tips 3
Allotment Tips
Backgammon Tips
Barbecue Tips
Beer Tips
Biscuit Tips
Bread Tips
Bridge Tips
Cake Baking Tips
Cake Decorating Tips
Cheese Tips
Chefs' Tips
Chess Tips
Chocolate Tips
Christmas Aga Tips
Chutney and Pickle Tips
Cleaning Tips
Cocktail Tips
Coffee Tips
Cupcake Tips
Curry Tips
Fishing Tips
Fly Fishing Tips
Frugal Tips
Gardening Tips
Golf Tips
Green Tips
Grow Your Own Tips
Herb Tips
Houseplant Tips
Ice Cream Tips
Jam Tips
Kitten Tips
Macaroon Tips
Marmite Tips
Olive Oil Tips
Pasta Tips
Poker Tips
Puppy Tips
Rayburn Tips
Seafood Tips
Spice Tips
Tea Tips
Toast Tips
Travel Tips
Whisky Tips
Wine Tips
Vinegar Tips